Cornerstones of Freedom

The White House

Deborah Kent

CHILDRENS PRESS®
CHICAGO

Library of Congress Cataloging-in-Publication Data

Kent, Deborah.
  The White House / by Deborah Kent.
    p. cm. – (Cornerstones of freedom)
  ISB 0-516-06684-6
  1. White House (Washington, D.C.)–Juvenile literature.
2. Washington (D.C.)–Buildings, structures, etc.–Juvenile
literature. [1. White House (Washington, D.C.)
2. Presidents.] I. Title. II. Series.
F204.W5K46   1994
973'.099–dc20
                                94-9489
                          CIP
                          AC

The planks of the makeshift bridge rang hollowly underfoot as President John Adams crossed above the rubble-strewn yard to the front door of his new home. It was November 1800, and the President's House had been under construction for eight years. Now John Adams, the nation's second president, could move in at last.

John Adams

When the president arrived, the mansion was barely livable. Littered with bricks, stones, and bits of lumber, the yard was so muddy that a temporary bridge had been built to keep the president's feet dry. Inside, half the rooms were still unplastered. The roof leaked, and the bathroom was a three-seated outhouse. Two weeks after her arrival, the president's wife, Abigail Adams, wrote, "The house is made habitable, but there is not a single apartment finished; and the great unfinished audience room [the East Room] I make a drying-room of, to hang up the clothes in."

Abigail Adams

Incomplete though it was, the President's House was the largest mansion in the new

Laundry is hung in the empty East Room as First Lady Abigail Adams looks on with her granddaughter.

American nation. It boasted thirty-six rooms on three floors, as well as a full basement with a vaulted stone ceiling. The stonework above the doors and windows was carved with intricate patterns of chains, leaves, and flowers.

The mansion was intended to serve not only as the president's home and workplace, but also as a center for public gatherings. A broad corridor ran the length of the first floor, opening onto five magnificent state rooms designed for receptions, formal dinners, and official ceremonies. One of these rooms, later called the Blue Room, was oval in shape, giving the house a unique profile.

George Washington, the nation's first president, had envisioned a much grander mansion. He had approved the design for a "Presidential Palace" created by French surveyor and architect Charles Pierre L'Enfant. L'Enfant planned a structure of solid stone, measuring 700 feet in length—longer than two football fields set end to end. The Presidential Palace was to be the apex of the glorious federal city that L'Enfant meant to create. The new capital of the United States, named for the first president, would be a city of parks, fountains, monuments, tree-lined boulevards, and splendid public buildings. Its grandeur would challenge the most beautiful

L'Enfant (inset) mapped out a detailed grid of city blocks for the capital city.

In the late 1790s, Washington was still a small city surrounded by wilderness.

cities in all Europe. The site of this dreamed-of magnificence was a patch of swampy land on the northern bank of the Potomac River. The tract was purchased from the state of Maryland to accommodate the federal city.

"The public buildings, in size, form, and elegance, should look beyond the present day," Washington wrote to the three commissioners whom he appointed to oversee the project. "For the President's House I would also design a building which should look forward."

L'Enfant was a brilliant architect, but he could be stubborn and demanding. He quarreled endlessly with the commissioners, asking for more and more money to complete his projects. At last, in February 1792, Washington reluctantly decided that L'Enfant's services must come to an end.

L'Enfant's successors carried out many of his original ideas for the capital city. But his design for the Presidential Palace was impossibly grand for the struggling young nation. Besides, many American leaders hoped to get away from the

The city of Washington, D.C., has grown around the White House very much as Pierre L'Enfant envisioned.

Two of architect James Hoban's designs for the President's House

aristocratic splendor of Europe. They wanted a President's House that would reflect the spirit of democracy—a house with both dignity and simplicity.

On March 14, 1792, the Washington commissioners placed the following notice in newspapers around the country: "A premium of $500 . . . will be given to a person who, before the fifteenth day of July next, shall produce the most approved plan for a Presidential House to be erected in this city." George Washington was to be the final judge.

By July 15, the commissioners received nine entries. Almost without hesitation, Washington selected the drawings of a three-story house fronted by a graceful columned portico. It was only one-third the size of L'Enfant's palace, but it had the classical columns and stonework he deeply admired. The plan had been submitted by a promising young architect named James Hoban.

Hoban was born to a large, impoverished family in rural Ireland. Through talent and perseverance, he managed to study architecture in Dublin. In 1785 he moved to America, hoping to make his fortune there. Winning the competition to design the President's House in 1792 was the opportunity he needed. He would work on the mansion and other federal buildings for the next thirty-nine years.

A view of the President's House only a few years after construction was completed

Much of the early work on the President's House was carried out by slaves, who were rented from their masters in Maryland and Virginia. As time passed, Hoban relied more heavily on foreign-born craftsmen. Colin Williamson of Scotland became his master stonemason. Williamson was gruff and often ill-tempered, but he set the highest standards for himself and for his workers. At quarries in Virginia, forty miles from the building site, he studied each sandstone block and numbered it according to its intended position in the mansion's walls.

By the winter of 1793, the basement was complete. Its walls were three feet thick and thirteen feet high. Its ceiling had massive stone arches designed to bear the weight of the finished mansion. But the construction costs were going beyond the commissioners' budget. Once again, President Washington saw his plans pared down by practical necessity. Instead of a mansion of solid stone, he was forced to accept a brick structure with an outer facing of stonework.

Slowly, over eight long years, the President's House took shape. George Washington did not live to see its completion; he died in 1799. But at last, in November 1800, President John Adams moved into the unfinished, echo-filled mansion. With him came wagonloads of furniture and government documents from Philadelphia, which had served as the nation's temporary capital. Adams also brought the first item purchased specifically for the President's House—a larger-than-life portrait of George Washington by noted American painter Gilbert Stuart.

John Adams lived in the President's House for only four months, and he was never comfortable there. Yet he approached it with reverence, awed by the nation's unknown future. On his first night in the mansion, he wrote, "I pray

The famous George Washington portrait by artist Gilbert Stuart

Intricate decoration highlights the exterior walls of the White House

Thomas Jefferson

heaven to bestow the best of blessings on this house, and all that shall hereafter inhabit it. May none but honest and wise men ever rule under this roof."

Thomas Jefferson enthusiastically took up work on the house when he became president in 1801. He added elaborate interior carvings of wreaths and ivy leaves, and laid out extensive gardens on the slope from the house to the river. He believed that the President's House belonged to the American people. Twice a year, on New Year's Day and the Fourth of July, he invited the public to a reception, complete with a concert by the Marine Corps Band. Throughout the year, visitors were welcome to tour the elegant state rooms on the first floor. Jefferson even set up a small museum to display plant specimens, animal skins, and Native American crafts from the nation's little-known western territories. One explorer, Zebulon Pike, donated two grizzly cubs, which wrestled and played in a pen just outside the house's north entrance.

By the time James Madison took office in 1809, the President's House was ready for entertaining on a grand scale. Madison's wife, Dolley, delighted in hosting elegant balls and banquets. During the Madison years, the President's House acquired a new nickname. Because of the coats of whitewash applied to its sandstone exterior, it became known as the White House.

In 1812, war erupted between the United States and Great Britain, as the two nations struggled for supremacy on the high seas. In August 1814, British troops landed on the shores of Chesapeake Bay and defeated American forces at Bladensburg, Maryland. At the White House, First Lady Dolley Madison waited anxiously for her husband, who had ridden out to watch the fighting. On August 24, hoping that the president and his party would soon return, Mrs. Madison ordered a midday meal for thirty-five people. Years later, Paul Jennings, who was a slave at the White House in 1814, described the scene in his autobiography.

James (top) and Dolley (bottom) Madison

This painting depicts Dolley Madison saving the portrait of George Washington before fleeing the White House.

"I set the tables myself, and brought up the ale, cider, and wine. At just about three o'clock, a rider pounded up the White House driveway, waving his hat and shouting." The rider was a messenger from the president, with orders that Washington must be evacuated at once. The British were on their way.

As servants piled trunks of valuables into wagons, Dolley Madison penned a few hasty lines to her sister. "Our kind friend Mr. Carroll has come to hasten my departure, and is in a very bad humor with me because I insist on waiting until the large picture of Mr. Washington is secured, and it requires to be unscrewed from the wall. This process was found to be too

tedious for these perilous moments. I have
ordered the frame to be broken and the canvas
taken out."

Late that evening, 150 British sailors marched
through the streets of the deserted capital.
Boldly, they entered the White House, gobbled
the meal that still waited in the abandoned
dining room, and burned much of the furniture.
As they left the house, they hurled dozens of
lighted torches in through the windows. "The
whole building was wrapped in flames and
smoke," wrote one eyewitness. "The spectators
stood in awful silence. The city was light, and

Washington burns as the British invade in 1814.

After the British invasion, the White House still stood, but it was heavily damaged by fire.

the heavens reddened with the blaze."

When the British finally left Washington, the White House, the Capitol, and nearly every other government building lay in ashes. The destruction of the White House was an especially heavy blow to the nation's morale. But despite the attack on the capital, the United States had the final victory in the war. In 1815, the commissioners of Washington hired James Hoban to restore the White House. Only the basement, built of solid stone, had survived unharmed. Some walls had to be entirely demolished and rebuilt. On the north side, Hoban could preserve little but the front door with its intricate carvings and its columned portico.

When President James Monroe moved into the restored White House in 1817, the plaster

James Monroe

was wet, the woodwork was unpainted, and the floors were bare. At once he set to work, ordering crates of elegant new furniture from France. On New Year's Day, he held the traditional public reception. Like the spirit of the nation itself, the White House had survived the devastation of war.

Andrew Jackson

Public revelry at the White House got out of hand when Andrew Jackson was inaugurated as the nation's seventh president in 1829. All of the earlier presidents had come from wealthy, established families, while Jackson was a homespun frontiersman. At his inaugural reception, his boisterous admirers smashed

As Andrew Jackson's inaugural party got out of hand, the drunken partyers began damaging the White House and its contents.

Some of the White House's valuable china, crystal, and silver

chandeliers, shattered expensive china, and stained satin cushions with their muddy boots. In its excitement, the crowd nearly crushed the president to death. Aides finally helped him escape through a window to safety.

In March 1861, a tall, homely lawyer from Illinois named Abraham Lincoln became America's sixteenth president. Within weeks, the nation plunged into a brutal civil war that pitted North against South. Through the terrible war years, Lincoln saw the White House as a cherished symbol of national unity. He continued to hold receptions and balls, and he purchased an assortment of handsome new furniture. But he was furious when his wife, Mary Todd Lincoln, exceeded their limited budget to buy a magnificent canopied bed. "It would stink in the nostrils of the American people," he roared, "to have it said that the President of the United States approved a

Abraham and Mary Todd Lincoln

bill . . . for flubdubs for this damned old house, when the soldiers cannot have blankets!" Today, the "Lincoln Bed" is one of the most highly prized White House treasures.

On April 9, 1865, the war finally came to an end. At last the suffering nation could begin to heal its wounds. Lincoln was exhausted, but determined to show the people that life could go on. On the night of April 14, he and his wife attended a play at Washington's Ford's Theatre. Suddenly a shot rang out, and the president slumped forward. An assassin, a prominent actor named John Wilkes Booth, had crept into the presidential box and fired from pointblank

The Lincoln Bedroom is still in use as a guest room. The famous Lincoln Bed is eight feet long.

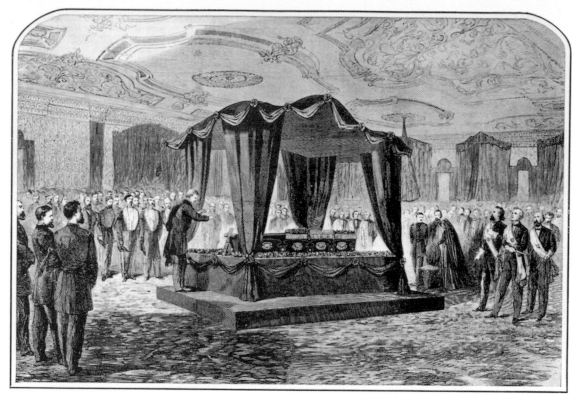

President Lincoln's funeral in the East Room of the White House

range. Lincoln never regained consciousness, and died early the following morning.

As the nation wept, the White House was draped inside and out with black crepe. Even the mirrors were covered, and the chandeliers were wrapped in black cloth. Thousands of silent mourners formed a line more than a mile long. They filed into the White House and past the president's coffin. It rested on a sixteen-foot canopied platform, or catafalque, in the East Room. After the funeral service, Lincoln's body was placed on a hearse drawn by six white horses and carried down Pennsylvania Avenue to the Capitol. From there it was loaded onto a special

funeral train for the long journey back to
Springfield, Illinois, its final resting place.

Mad with grief, Mary Todd Lincoln remained
in her room at the White House until May 22.
Later, she wrote, "All the sorrows of my life
occurred there, and that whited sepulchre
[tomb] broke my heart."

Like Lincoln, many U.S. presidents have grown
exhausted and even ill under the burden of their
responsibilities. Theodore Roosevelt and his
family, however, thoroughly enjoyed their years
in the White House. The five Roosevelt children
roller-skated in the East Room, walked on stilts
in the gardens, and kept a menagerie of pets.

*Theodore Roosevelt and his family made a home out of the White House
and its grounds. The children kept a variety of pets, including Eli,
Theodore Jr.'s macaw (left), and Algonquin, Quentin's pony (right).*

Part of the additional West Wing was the Oval Office, where the president works. Facing the president's desk is a painting of George Washington.

When the Roosevelts arrived in 1901, the White House was showing its age. It did not have enough bathrooms, closets, or fire exits. In many rooms, the floors sagged dangerously. Theodore Roosevelt made plans to renovate the entire mansion. With the help of Charles McKim, a New York architect, he redesigned the second-floor living quarters, updated the plumbing and wiring, and enlarged the State Dining Room. Because the cramped second-floor quarters were no longer adequate for the offices of the president and his staff, an executive wing—called the West Wing—was also added to the house. Under Roosevelt, the President's House was officially renamed the White House.

In the twentieth century, the nation endured two world wars and a catastrophic economic depression. Through these ordeals, the White House remained a symbol of unity and survival. During World War II, military guards patrolled the White House grounds, and President Franklin D. Roosevelt had a bomb shelter constructed beneath the basement. He also enlarged the West Wing and added an indoor swimming pool there. Years before he became president, Roosevelt had had polio, and he needed the pool to exercise his legs.

Despite Theodore Roosevelt's 1902 renovations, the White House continued to deteriorate. Its

Franklin Delano Roosevelt

The White House swimming pool

23

beams and inner walls had become riddled with holes for plumbing, heating, and electrical systems that James Hoban had never envisioned. The added weight of pipes, ducts, and wiring put tremendous strain on the original structure. In 1948, President Harry S. Truman wrote in his diary, "[My daughter] Margaret's sitting-room floor broke but didn't fall through the family dining-room ceiling. They propped it up and fixed it. Now my bathroom is about to fall into the Red Parlor. They won't let me sleep in my bedroom or use the bath." One architect told the president, "The mansion is standing up purely by habit."

Workmen repair a ceiling during the White House renovation of the late 1940s.

The renovation gave the White House a fresh look both inside and out.

Architect Lorenzo S. Winslow was in charge of the massive project.

The White House was in such disrepair that many engineers advised that it should be demolished. But Truman was deeply committed to preserving the mansion. In December 1948, he and his family moved across Pennsylvania Avenue to Blair House, and a vast reconstruction project was begun. For three years, under the direction of architect Lorenzo S. Winslow, workers stripped the White House down to its original brick walls, then meticulously rebuilt it room by room. Winslow reinstalled as much of the original woodwork as possible, and replaced many of the house's marble mantelpieces. The entire structure was reinforced with 800 tons of steel beams and girders.

By March 1952, the White House had been completely refurbished. The basement, or ground floor, was almost unchanged, and the original outer walls still stood firm. But nearly everything else had been rebuilt. Truman had also added a second-floor balcony behind the columns of the South Portico.

Ten years later, in February 1962, the American public was permitted to explore the renewed White House through a televised tour hosted by Jacqueline Kennedy, the wife of President John F. Kennedy. Mrs. Kennedy had taken a keen interest in the house's interior decoration. She believed that every item in the White House should be there for a historical reason, and encouraged the purchase and donation of furniture and artwork with historical significance.

On November 22, 1963, the world was stunned by the assassination of President Kennedy in

Dallas, Texas. Jacqueline Kennedy requested that her husband's funeral be modeled after that of President Lincoln. Once again, the White House was hung with black crepe, and the chandeliers, mirrors, and furniture were wrapped in the cloth of mourning. Like Abraham Lincoln, John F. Kennedy lay in state on a catafalque in the East Room before his body was carried to the Capitol.

After resigning from office, Richard Nixon delivered an emotional farewell speech to the White House staff on August 9, 1974.

In 1974, the White House witnessed yet another momentous drama. On August 9, from the Oval Office in the Executive Office Building, President Richard M. Nixon announced his resignation. Nixon's administration had been tarnished by a series of political scandals, and he faced almost certain impeachment. Most of the evidence against him was based on conversations that he had secretly taped in the Oval Office.

Each president has left his unique mark on the White House, just as he has touched the nation itself. Most have added paintings, books, dinnerware, or furniture—all remembrances of a particular time in history. Many presidents and their families have found forgotten treasures in the house's storerooms, and put them on public display. In 1993, First Lady Hillary Rodham

The State Dining Room seats up to 140 guests for formal dinners. Hanging above the mantel is a painting of Abraham Lincoln.

Clinton described her goal as "preservation and restoration, not redecoration—furthering the historic mission of the house."

Every year, more than one million people visit the White House, which stands on 18 acres of land at 1600 Pennsylvania Avenue in Washington, D.C. Although it has never reached the dimensions that L'Enfant intended, the house has grown considerably since John Adams lived there in 1800. Graceful terraces connect the main building with the West Wing and the East Wing. The West Wing, or Executive Office Building, contains the Oval Office, where the president conducts official business. It also houses presidential staff offices and various meeting rooms, including the Cabinet Room. The East Wing houses the offices of social secretaries, military aides, and other White House staff members.

The White House now has 132 rooms on four levels, including the ground floor, or basement. The president's living quarters and private dining room are on the second floor. The third floor contains guest rooms and living quarters for some staff members. Store rooms, laundry facilities, and an enormous kitchen are located on the ground floor. The White House also has a private bowling alley and a movie theater.

Some of the many elegant rooms in the White House include the Red Room (top); the Diplomatic Reception Room (middle), which used to be a boiler room before it was renovated; and the oval-shaped Blue Room (left).

Top: The State Dining Room Bottom: The Green Room, where a painting of an elderly Benjamin Franklin hangs above the fireplace

Five of the White House's rooms are open to the public. These are the state rooms along the main corridor on the first floor: the State Dining Room, the Red Room, the Blue Room, the Green Room, and the East Room.

The State Dining Room is the setting for the president's formal banquets. According to strict White House protocol, the president is always the last person to be seated. Visitors to the dining room can read John Adams's famous prayer inscribed on the mantel above the fireplace.

The Red Room is decorated with long, gold-trimmed curtains of red silk. In this room, the First Lady receives guests. The oval Blue Room is the mansion's main reception room. There visitors may admire some of the furniture that James Monroe ordered from France after the White House was burned. The walls of the Green Room, another reception room, are covered with light-green silk. The East Room is the largest and most formal room in the White House. It is eighty feet long and has a twenty-two-foot ceiling. In this room hangs the portrait of George Washington that Dolley Madison rescued from the British. Visitors may pause to remember Abraham Lincoln and John F. Kennedy, the fallen leaders who lay in this room awaiting burial.

President Woodrow Wilson once wrote of the White House: "In this place, time is not

measured by weeks or months or years, but
by deep human experiences." The White House
has seen the joys and sorrows, triumphs and
humiliations of more than forty American
presidents. In a sense, it is a time capsule.
Its furniture and carvings, paintings and statuary
are priceless reminders of the nation's rich and
often tumultuous history. As Theodore Roosevelt
told Congress in 1903, "The White House is
the property of the nation. It is a good thing to
preserve such buildings as historic monuments
which keep alive our sense of continuity with
our nation's past."

INDEX (Page numbers in boldface indicate illustrations.)

Adams, Abigail, 3, **3**, **4**
Adams, John, 3, **3**, 11, 28, 30
Blair House, 25
Blue Room, 4, **29**, 30
Booth, John Wilkes, 19
Cabinet Room, 29
Civil War (American), 18, 19
Clinton, Hillary Rodham, 27–28
Diplomatic Reception Room, **29**
Dublin, Ireland, 9
East Room, **4**, 20, **20**, 27, 30
Ford's Theatre, 19
Green Room, 30, **30**
Hoban, James, 9–19, 16, 24
Jackson, Andrew, 17–18, **17**
Jefferson, Thomas, 12, **12**, 13
Jennings, Paul, 13
Kennedy, Jacqueline, 26, **26**, 27
Kennedy, John F., 26–27, 30
L'Enfant, Charles Pierre, 5, **5**, 7, 9, 28
Lincoln, Abraham, 18, **18**, 19–20, **20**, 27, 30

Lincoln Bed, 18, 19, **19**
Lincoln, Mary Todd, 18, **18**, 21
Madison, Dolley, 13, **13**, 14, **14**, 30
Madison, James, 13, **13**
Marine Corps Band, 12
Maryland, 6, 10
Monroe, James, 16, **16**, 30
Nixon, Richard M., 27, **27**
Oval Office, **22**, 27, 28
Philadelphia, Pennsylvania, 11
Pike, Zebulon, 13
Potomac River, 6
Red Room, **29**, 30
Roosevelt, Franklin Delano, 23, **23**
Roosevelt, Quentin, 21
Roosevelt, Theodore, 21, 22, 31
Roosevelt, Theodore, Jr., **21**
State Dining Room, 28, 30, **30**
Stuart, Gilbert, 11
Truman, Harry S., 24, 25, 26
War of 1812, 13
Washington, D.C., 5–6, **5**, **6**, **7**, 9

Washington, George, 4–5, 6, 7, 9, 11, **11**, 30
West Wing, 22, 23
White House
  British invasion of, 14–16
  construction of, 10–11, 12
  design of, 5, 7, **8**, 9, **12**
  funerals at, 20, **20**, 27
  named White House, 13, 22
  pets at, 21, **21**
  as President's House, 3–4, **4**, 9, **10**, 11
  renovations of, 22, 23, 24–26, **24**, **25**
  restoration of, 16–17
  rooms in, **19**, **22**, **28**, **29**, **30**
  swimming pool, 23, **23**
  wings of, 28–29
Williamson, Colin, 10
Wilson, Woodrow, 30–31
Winslow, Lorenzo S., 25, **25**
World War II, 23

PHOTO CREDITS

Cover, ©Dennis O'Clair/Tony Stone Images, Inc.; 1, Photri; 2, ©Mae Scanlan; 3 (top), Stock Montage, Inc.; 3 (bottom), Library of Congress; 4, ©White House Historical Association, photograph by National Geographic Society; 5 (top), Library of Congress; 5 (bottom), 6, North Wind Picture Archives; 7, Photri; 8 (top), ©White House Historical Association/ Massachusetts Historical Society; 8 (bottom) ©White House Historical Association/Maryland Historical Society; 10, Bettmann Archive; 11, ©White House Historical Association, photograph by National Geographic Society; 12 (top), ©White House Historical Association; 12 (left), AP/Wide World; 13 (top), North Wind Picture Archives; 13 (center), Stock Montage, Inc.; 14, ©White House Historical Association, photograph by National Geographic Society; 15, 16 (top), North Wind Picture Archives; 16 (bottom), 17 (top), Stock Montage, Inc.; 17 (bottom), ©White House Historical Association/ painted by ©Louis Glanzman; 18 (both photos), AP/Wide World; 19, Photri; 20, North Wind Picture Archives; 21 (both photos), Library of Congress; 22, SuperStock International; 23 (both photos), 24 (both photos), 25 (left, bottom right), AP/Wide World; 25 (top right), UPI/Bettmann; 26, 27, AP/Wide World; 28, 29 (left, bottom right), Photri; 29 (top right), ©Cameramann International; 30 (top), Photri; 30 (bottom), ©Paul Gero/First Image West, Inc.; 31, ©Maxwell Mackenzie/Tony Stone Images, Inc.

Picture Identifications:
Page 1: The moon rises over Washington, D.C.; towering over the White House is the Washington Monument, and the Jefferson Memorial is visible to the right.
Page 31: Lafayette Square, with the White House visible in the background

Project Editors: Shari Joffe and Mark Friedman
Design: Beth Herman Design Associates
Photo Research: Jan Izzo
Cornerstones of Freedom Logo: David Cunningham

ABOUT THE AUTHOR

Deborah Kent grew up in Little Falls, New Jersey, and received her B.A. from Oberlin College. She earned a master's degree in social work from Smith College, and worked for four years at the University Settlement House on New York's Lower East Side.

Ms. Kent left social work to begin a career in writing. She published her first novel, *Belonging*, while living in San Miguel de Allende, Mexico. She has written a dozen novels for young adults, as well as numerous nonfiction titles for children. She lives in Chicago with her husband and their daughter Janna.